THE HEALING TOUCH OF NATURE

AN INTRODUCTION TO NATUROPATHY

DR. MINAKSHI BANSAL

DEDICATION

To the healing power of nature, the wisdom of our ancestors, and the resilience of the human spirit.

ⴘⴘⴘ

Contents

Contents

Prayer

"Om Bhadram Karnebhih Shrinuyama Devah

Bhadram Pashyemakshabhiryajatrah

Sthirairangais Tushtuvamsastanubhih

Vyashema Devahitam Yadayuh

Svasti Na Indro Vriddhashravah

Svasti Nah Pusha Vishwavedah

Svasti Nastarkshyo Arishtanemih

Svasti No Brihaspatir Dadhatu

Om Shantih Shantih Shantih"

This mantra is a prayer for universal well-being, invoking the blessings of various deities for protection, health, and happiness. It emphasizes the importance of experiencing the auspicious through all senses and living a life aligned with divine purpose. The repetition of "Shantih" at the end signifies a deep desire for peace in the individual, the environment, and the universe at large. This mantra is often recited as a prayer for peace, prosperity, and the physical and spiritual well-being of all beings.

About The Author

This book represents the culmination of extensive research and meticulous analysis, incorporating a diverse range of sources, including numerous books, scholarly studies, and personal experiences. Additionally, I have scoured various websites to gather relevant information and data essential for the compilation of this work. I have taken every precaution to ensure the accuracy of the information presented and have diligently cited all sources to acknowledge their contributions.

From her earliest days, Minakshi was distinguished by an insatiable appetite for reading. Her literary universe was inhabited by characters and narratives that spanned ethical tales, motivational and inspirational stories, and the mythic parables imbued with life lessons. This voracious reading habit was not merely for personal edification but was driven by a desire to distill and disseminate the essence of these narratives to foster the development of students and peers alike. She was particularly captivated by the lives and teachings of historical figures and spiritual leaders such as Adi Shankaracharya, Swami Vivekananda, Dr. APJ Abdul Kalam, Mahamana Pandit Madan Mohan Malviya, Mahatma Gandhi, Sardar Vallabhai Patel, and Vinoba Bhave, among others. Their philosophies and life stories fueled her ambition to embody their ideals of resilience, selflessness, and relentless pursuit of knowledge.

Dr. Minakshi's academic and practical engagement with psychology has been equally noteworthy. As a research scholar, her focus has been on exploring the intricate tapestry of the human psyche, aiming to unlock the potential for psychological well-being and societal harmony. Her scholarly work is complemented by her active involvement in social work, where she employs her academic insights to make tangible differences in the lives of the underprivileged. Her endeavours in social work are characterized by an innovative approach that combines traditional wisdom with contemporary psychological practices to address the multifaceted challenges faced by these communities.

Her artistic talents, another facet of her diverse capabilities, are not merely a personal passion but also serve as a medium through which she communicates and connects with others. Her art, rich in symbolism and emotional depth, reflects her philosophical inquiries and social concerns, offering viewers a glimpse into the breadth of her intellect and the depth of her compassion.

In addition to her contributions to the arts and social sciences, Dr. Minakshi has embraced the healing arts of Pranic Healing, mastering the techniques developed by Master Choa Kok Sui. This practice, which focuses on the manipulation of Prana or life energy to heal the body and aura, has been both a personal journey of discovery and a means through which she extends her healing touch to others. Her proficiency in Pranic Healing is complemented by her advocacy and teaching of various forms of meditation aimed at rejuvenation, personal betterment, and the cultivation of harmony within individuals and communities alike.

Dr. Minakshi's life is a narrative of relentless pursuit, not just of personal achievement but of the upliftment and empowerment of society at large. Her diverse interests and talents—spanning the arts, literature, psychology, and the healing practices—converge on a singular path of service. She embodies the spirit of the luminaries who inspired her, channelling their legacy through her actions and teachings. Through her books, art, and social initiatives, she continues to inspire a new generation to embark on their own journeys of self-discovery, resilience, and altruism.

Her commitment to social betterment, particularly her focus on uplifting underprivileged children, reflects a deep understanding of the transformative potential of education and personal development. By integrating her knowledge of psychology, her artistic sensibilities, and her healing practices, Dr. Bansal has developed a holistic approach to social work that addresses both the immediate needs and the long-term well-being of the communities she serves.

As an author, Dr. Minakshi's writings offer a blend of inspirational insights, practical wisdom, and reflective contemplations drawn from her extensive reading and life experiences. Her books serve as a guide for those seeking to navigate the complexities of life with grace, resilience, and purpose. Through her narratives, she extends an invitation to her readers to explore the depths of their own potential and to contribute meaningfully to the collective well-being of society.

In Dr. Minakshi Bansal, we find a remarkable synthesis of the artist, the scholar, the healer, and the social activist. Her life's work stands as a beacon of hope and a source of inspiration for individuals seeking to make a difference in the world. Her story is a compelling reminder of the power of individual action, rooted in compassion and driven by a profound commitment to the betterment of humanity. Dr. Minakshi's legacy is not just in the tangible outcomes of her efforts but in the enduring spirit of inquiry, empathy, and service that she embodies.

Preface

In a world often consumed by the frenetic pace of modern life, it is easy to lose sight of the simple yet profound truths that nurture our health and well-being. We have become disconnected from the natural world, from the rhythms of the seasons, from the wisdom of our bodies. We have turned to quick fixes and synthetic solutions, seeking relief from ailments without addressing the underlying causes.

It is in this context that I offer this book as a gentle invitation to rediscover the healing touch of nature. Naturopathy, a holistic system of medicine rooted in ancient wisdom and modern science, offers a pathway to vibrant health and well-being by harnessing the innate power of nature to heal and restore.

In this book, I will guide you through the fundamental principles of naturopathy, exploring its philosophy, its practices, and its potential to transform your health. We will delve into the healing power of nutrition, the gentle remedies of herbal medicine, the restorative properties of water, and the importance of cultivating a healthy mind-body connection. We will also explore the role of sleep, sunlight, air quality, emotional well-being, spiritual connection, community, and sustainable living in creating a life of optimal health.

This book is not a comprehensive guide to naturopathy, nor is it a substitute for professional medical advice. Rather, it is an introduction to the principles and practices of this ancient yet timeless healing art. It is my hope that this book will inspire you to explore the many ways in which nature can support your health and well-being, and to embrace a holistic approach to living that honors the interconnectedness of all things.

My own journey into the world of naturopathy began many years ago, when I was struggling with chronic health issues that conventional medicine had failed to address. I was tired, stressed, and disillusioned with the endless cycle of doctor's appointments and prescriptions. I knew there had to be a better way, a way to heal my body without further compromising it.

It was then that I discovered naturopathy. I was drawn to its holistic approach, its emphasis on natural remedies, and its focus on prevention. I began to incorporate naturopathic principles into my life, making changes to my diet, exercise routine, and stress management practices. Slowly but surely, I began to feel better. My energy levels increased, my mood improved, and my chronic symptoms began to subside.

I was so inspired by my own experience with naturopathy that I decided to study it formally. I enrolled in a naturopathic medical school and immersed myself in the study of natural medicine. After graduating, I opened my own practice and began helping others to discover the healing power of nature.

Over the years, I have had the privilege of working with countless individuals who have sought my help in their quest for health and well-being. I have witnessed firsthand the transformative power of naturopathy, and I am passionate about sharing this knowledge with others.

In writing this book, I have drawn upon my own experiences as a naturopathic doctor, as well as the wisdom of countless healers and teachers who have come before me. I have also incorporated the latest scientific research on natural medicine, ensuring that the information presented in this book is both accurate and up-to-date.

It is my sincere hope that this book will serve as a guide and inspiration for those who are seeking a more natural and holistic approach to health. May it empower you to take charge of your well-being, to connect with the healing power of nature, and to create a life that is vibrant, joyful, and fulfilling.

Dr. Minakshi Bansal
Social Activist
Ahmedabad, Gujarat, Bharat

ONE

NATUROPATHY: YOUR BODY'S INNATE WISDOM FOR HEALING.

In the heart of every living being lies an extraordinary capacity for self-repair and rejuvenation. This inherent wisdom, often overlooked in our modern world, is the cornerstone of naturopathy, a holistic system of medicine that honors the body's innate ability to heal itself. Naturopathy views the human body as a complex ecosystem, intricately connected to the natural world, and seeks to restore balance and harmony within this system through gentle, non-invasive therapies.

At its core, naturopathy embraces the principle of "Vis Medicatrix Naturae," which translates to "the healing power of nature." This philosophy recognizes that the body possesses an intrinsic intelligence that guides its healing processes.

Naturopaths believe that given the right conditions, the body can naturally ward off disease, repair damaged tissues, and maintain optimal health. This inherent wisdom is not a mystical force, but rather a symphony of biological processes working in concert to maintain equilibrium.

One of the fundamental tenets of naturopathy is the concept of treating the whole person, not just the symptoms of disease. Naturopaths recognize that physical, mental, emotional, and spiritual well-being are interconnected, and that imbalances in one area can manifest as dis-ease in another.

Therefore, naturopathic treatment plans address the root causes of illness, rather than simply suppressing symptoms. This approach often involves lifestyle modifications, dietary changes, herbal remedies, and other natural therapies that support the body's innate healing mechanisms.

Nutrition plays a pivotal role in naturopathic medicine. The adage "you are what you eat" holds profound truth, as the food we consume provides the building blocks for our cells and tissues. Naturopaths emphasize whole, unprocessed foods that nourish the body and support its natural functions.

A balanced diet rich in fruits, vegetables, whole grains, and lean protein provides essential vitamins, minerals, and antioxidants that bolster the immune system and promote optimal health. Additionally, naturopaths may recommend specific dietary modifications to address individual needs and health concerns.

Herbal medicine is another cornerstone of naturopathic practice. Plants have been used for medicinal purposes for centuries, and their therapeutic properties are well-documented. Naturopaths utilize a wide array of herbs to support various bodily functions, alleviate symptoms, and promote healing.

These remedies can be administered in various forms, including teas, tinctures, capsules, and topical preparations. Herbal medicine offers a gentle and effective alternative to pharmaceutical drugs, with fewer side effects and a focus on long-term wellness.

Hydrotherapy, the therapeutic use of water, is another valuable tool in the naturopath's arsenal. Water has a remarkable ability to soothe, cleanse, and revitalize the body. Naturopaths employ various hydrotherapy techniques, such as baths, showers, compresses, and wraps, to promote circulation, reduce inflammation, and enhance detoxification. Hydrotherapy can be particularly beneficial for conditions such as arthritis, muscle pain, and skin disorders.

The mind-body connection is a central theme in naturopathic medicine. Stress, anxiety, and negative emotions can wreak havoc on our health, suppressing the immune system and contributing to chronic disease. Naturopaths recognize the importance of cultivating a positive mindset and managing stress effectively.

Techniques such as meditation, yoga, deep breathing exercises, and mindfulness can help to calm the nervous system, reduce stress hormones, and promote relaxation. By fostering a healthy mind-body connection, we create an environment conducive to healing.

Detoxification is another important aspect of naturopathic practice. Our bodies are constantly exposed to environmental toxins, pollutants, and processed foods, which can accumulate over time and burden our organs.

Naturopaths utilize various methods to support the body's natural detoxification processes, including dietary changes, herbal remedies, and hydrotherapy. By eliminating toxins and supporting the organs of elimination, we allow the body to function optimally and promote healing.

Naturopathy is not a quick fix or a magic bullet. It is a journey of self-discovery and empowerment. Naturopaths work collaboratively with their patients, educating them about their health and empowering them to make informed choices. By understanding the principles of naturopathy and embracing its gentle therapies, we can tap into our body's innate wisdom and embark on a path toward lifelong wellness.

ԺԺԺ

Nature whispers its wisdom to those who listen. In every leaf, every flower, every gentle breeze, there lies a healing touch waiting to be discovered. Embrace the natural world, and let its rhythms guide you toward vibrant health.

TWO

NATURAL REMEDIES: HARNESSING NATURE'S MEDICINE CHEST

In the tapestry of human history, the use of natural remedies for healing and wellness is deeply interwoven. Long before the advent of modern pharmaceuticals, our ancestors turned to the earth's bounty for relief from ailments and to maintain their health. Nature, in its infinite wisdom, provides a vast and diverse medicine chest, brimming with plants, minerals, and other natural substances that possess remarkable therapeutic properties. Today, amidst the hustle and bustle of modern life, the allure of natural remedies continues to captivate those seeking holistic and sustainable approaches to health and well-being.

The concept of natural remedies encompasses a wide array of modalities, each drawing upon the inherent healing potential of nature's gifts. Herbal medicine, perhaps the most well-known form of natural remedy, utilizes the medicinal properties of plants to support the body's innate healing mechanisms. From soothing chamomile tea to invigorating ginseng root, the plant kingdom offers a vast array of remedies for various ailments, ranging from minor coughs and colds to chronic conditions such as arthritis and anxiety. Herbal remedies can be administered in various forms, including teas, tinctures, capsules, and topical preparations, making them accessible and adaptable to individual needs.

Essential oils, extracted from the aromatic compounds of plants, are another potent form of natural remedy. These highly concentrated oils are renowned for their therapeutic properties, which can be harnessed through inhalation, topical application, or diffusion. Lavender oil, for example, is celebrated for its calming and sleep-promoting effects, while peppermint oil is known for its ability to alleviate headaches and digestive discomfort. Essential oils offer a natural and often enjoyable way to support physical, emotional, and mental well-being.

Beyond plants, the natural world offers a wealth of other healing substances. Minerals, such as magnesium and zinc, are essential for countless bodily functions, from energy production to immune system support. Probiotics, beneficial bacteria that reside in our gut, play a crucial role in digestion, immune function, and overall health. These natural substances can be obtained through diet, supplements, or topical applications, providing a natural and often gentle approach to maintaining health and preventing disease.

The appeal of natural remedies lies not only in their effectiveness but also in their holistic approach to health. Unlike many conventional pharmaceuticals, which often target specific symptoms, natural remedies tend to address the root causes of illness, promoting overall balance and harmony within the body. They often work synergistically with the body's natural healing processes, supporting rather than suppressing its innate wisdom.

Moreover, natural remedies are often associated with fewer side effects than their pharmaceutical counterparts. This is not to say that natural remedies are without risk, as some can interact with medications or cause allergic reactions. However, when used responsibly and under the guidance of a qualified healthcare practitioner, natural remedies can offer a safe and effective alternative or complement to conventional medicine.

In an era of increasing environmental awareness, natural remedies also hold appeal for their sustainability and minimal impact on the planet. Many natural remedies are sourced from renewable resources, and their production often involves less energy and fewer harmful chemicals than the production of pharmaceuticals. This alignment with ecological principles resonates with those seeking to live in harmony with nature and minimize their environmental footprint.

The journey into the world of natural remedies is one of exploration, discovery, and empowerment. It is a journey that invites us to reconnect with the healing power of nature, to tap into the wisdom of our ancestors, and to embrace a holistic approach to health and well-being. Whether we seek relief from a specific ailment or simply wish to enhance our overall vitality, the natural world offers a treasure trove of remedies waiting to be discovered.

As we navigate the complexities of modern life, the allure of natural remedies remains as strong as ever. They offer a bridge between ancient wisdom and modern science, a path toward holistic healing and a reminder of our profound connection to the natural world. By harnessing the power of nature's medicine chest, we can nurture our bodies, minds, and spirits, and embark on a journey toward optimal health and well-being.

ppp

Your body is a temple, a sacred vessel with an innate capacity for healing. Nourish it with wholesome foods, move it with joy, and quiet the mind to unleash its full potential for vitality and well-being.

THREE

HOLISTIC HEALTH: NURTURING MIND, BODY, AND SPIRIT.

In the symphony of human existence, health is not merely the absence of disease but a harmonious interplay of mind, body, and spirit. Holistic health, a philosophy deeply rooted in ancient wisdom and modern science, embraces this interconnectedness, recognizing that true well-being encompasses not only physical vitality but also mental clarity, emotional balance, and spiritual fulfillment. This comprehensive approach to health acknowledges that each of these dimensions influences and is influenced by the others, creating a dynamic and intricate tapestry of human experience.

At the heart of holistic health lies the understanding that the human being is not a collection of isolated parts but an integrated whole. The mind, with its thoughts, beliefs, and perceptions, profoundly impacts our physical and emotional states. Chronic stress, for example, can manifest as physical ailments such as headaches, digestive issues, and weakened immunity. Conversely, positive emotions like joy and gratitude can bolster the immune system and promote healing. The body, in turn, influences our mental and emotional states. Regular exercise not only strengthens muscles and bones but also releases endorphins, neurotransmitters that elevate mood and reduce stress. The spirit, often described as the essence of our being, provides meaning, purpose, and connection to something larger than ourselves. A sense of spiritual well-being can foster resilience in the face of adversity and contribute to overall life satisfaction.

Holistic health encompasses a wide array of practices and modalities, each designed to nurture and support the interconnectedness of mind, body, and spirit. Mindfulness, a practice rooted in ancient Buddhist traditions, involves paying non-judgmental attention to the present moment. This simple yet profound practice has been shown to reduce stress, improve focus, and enhance emotional regulation. Yoga, a mind-body practice that combines physical postures, breathwork, and meditation, offers a myriad of benefits for both physical and mental health. Regular yoga practice can increase flexibility, strength, and balance, while also promoting relaxation, stress reduction, and self-awareness.

Nutrition, a cornerstone of holistic health, recognizes that the food we consume not only fuels our bodies but also influences our moods, energy levels, and overall well-being. A balanced diet rich in whole, unprocessed foods provides the nutrients necessary for optimal physical and mental function. Conversely, a diet high in processed foods, sugar, and unhealthy fats can contribute to inflammation, fatigue, and mood swings. Holistic nutrition emphasizes the importance of mindful eating, savoring each bite, and listening to the body's hunger and fullness cues.

Physical activity, another essential component of holistic health, encompasses not only structured exercise but also movement integrated into daily life. Regular physical activity has been shown to reduce the risk of chronic diseases, improve cardiovascular health, and enhance mood and cognitive function. It can also serve as a form of meditation in motion, allowing us to connect with our bodies and cultivate a sense of presence.

In addition to these core practices, holistic health encompasses a wide range of complementary and alternative therapies, each offering unique benefits for mind, body, and spirit. Acupuncture, an ancient Chinese practice that involves inserting thin needles into specific points on the body, has been shown to be effective for pain relief, stress reduction, and various other conditions. Massage therapy, a hands-on healing modality, can promote relaxation, reduce muscle tension, and improve circulation. Herbal remedies, derived from plants, have been used for centuries to support various bodily functions and promote healing.

The journey toward holistic health is a lifelong endeavor, one that involves self-awareness, commitment, and a willingness to explore different modalities and practices. It is not about achieving perfection but about striving for balance and harmony in all aspects of our being. By nurturing our minds, bodies, and spirits, we can unlock our full potential for health, happiness, and well-being. We can cultivate resilience in the face of challenges, find meaning and purpose in our lives, and live each day with vitality and gratitude. Holistic health is a gift we give ourselves, a testament to our inherent wisdom and our profound connection to the world around us.

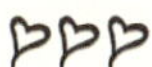

The earth's medicine chest is overflowing with gentle yet powerful remedies. From soothing herbs to revitalizing essential oils, nature provides us with everything we need to heal and thrive.

FOUR

VITAL FORCE: AWAKENING YOUR INNER HEALING ENERGY.

Within every living being, a vibrant and dynamic energy pulsates, a life force that animates our cells, fuels our organs, and orchestrates the intricate dance of our biological processes. This vital force, also known as chi, prana, or simply life energy, is the essence of our existence, the spark that ignites our physical, mental, emotional, and spiritual well-being. In the realm of holistic health, the concept of vital force holds profound significance, as it represents our innate capacity for self-healing and regeneration.

The vital force is not a mystical or esoteric concept but a fundamental principle recognized by various cultures and healing traditions throughout history. Traditional Chinese Medicine, for example, views chi as the energy that flows through meridians, or energy channels, in the body, maintaining balance and harmony. Ayurveda, the ancient Indian system of medicine, emphasizes the importance of prana, the vital breath that sustains life and nourishes the body's tissues. In many indigenous cultures, the concept of life energy is deeply intertwined with their spiritual beliefs and practices.

While the terminology and interpretations may vary, the essence of the vital force remains consistent: it is the animating principle that distinguishes living beings from inanimate objects. This life force is not confined to the physical body but permeates our entire being, influencing our thoughts, emotions, and spiritual connection. When our vital force is strong and vibrant, we experience optimal health, vitality, and well-being. However, when this energy becomes depleted or blocked, we may experience physical ailments, emotional distress, or a sense of spiritual disconnection.

The good news is that we have the power to awaken and cultivate our inner healing energy. By tapping into the vital force, we can enhance our body's natural ability to heal itself, restore balance and harmony, and experience greater vitality and well-being. There are many ways to awaken and cultivate the vital force, and the most effective approach will vary depending on individual needs and preferences.

One of the most fundamental ways to nurture the vital force is through mindful breathing. The breath is the bridge between the physical and the subtle realms of our being, and conscious breathing can help us to connect with the vital force that flows through us. Deep, diaphragmatic breathing, for example, can calm the nervous system, reduce stress, and promote relaxation, all of which support the flow of vital energy.

Another powerful way to awaken the vital force is through movement. Exercise, yoga, tai chi, and qigong are all practices that can stimulate the flow of energy in the body, increase circulation, and promote overall health and well-being. These practices not only strengthen the physical body but also cultivate mental clarity, emotional balance, and spiritual connection.

Nutrition also plays a crucial role in nourishing the vital force. A diet rich in whole, unprocessed foods, including fruits, vegetables, whole grains, and healthy fats, provides the essential nutrients that the body needs to thrive. Conversely, a diet high in processed foods, sugar, and unhealthy fats can deplete the vital force and contribute to various health problems.

In addition to these foundational practices, there are many other ways to awaken and cultivate the vital force. Meditation, visualization, and energy healing modalities such as Reiki can help to clear blockages in the energy field and promote a harmonious flow of energy. Spending time in nature, connecting with loved ones, and engaging in creative pursuits can also nourish the vital force and enhance our overall well-being.

The journey of awakening the vital force is a personal one, and it requires commitment, self-awareness, and a willingness to explore different modalities and practices. By cultivating a deeper understanding of this powerful life energy and incorporating practices that support its flow, we can unlock our innate capacity for healing, transformation, and well-being. The vital force is a gift, a wellspring of energy that resides within each of us, waiting to be discovered and nurtured. By tapping into this inner power, we can embark on a path of vibrant health, vitality, and spiritual fulfillment.

ppp

True health is not merely the absence of disease but a harmonious balance of mind, body, and spirit. Cultivate inner peace, embrace positive emotions, and nurture your spiritual connection for a life of wholeness and fulfillment.

FIVE

PREVENTION: BUILDING LIFELONG WELLNESS HABITS.

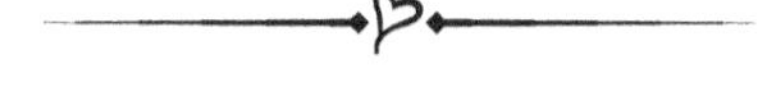

In the pursuit of optimal health, prevention reigns supreme. The adage "an ounce of prevention is worth a pound of cure" holds profound wisdom, emphasizing the importance of proactively nurturing our well-being rather than simply reacting to illness. The foundation of prevention lies in the cultivation of lifelong wellness habits, a series of intentional choices and practices that empower us to take charge of our health and create a vibrant, thriving life. These habits are not quick fixes or temporary solutions but rather sustainable lifestyle choices that become ingrained in our daily routines, supporting our physical, mental, emotional, and spiritual well-being throughout the years.

At the heart of preventive health lies the concept of self-care. Self-care is not merely indulgence but a fundamental act of self-preservation. It involves listening to our bodies, honoring our needs, and making choices that support our overall well-being. This encompasses a wide range of practices, from getting enough sleep and eating nourishing foods to managing stress and engaging in activities that bring us joy. When we prioritize self-care, we create a solid foundation for health and resilience, empowering ourselves to navigate life's challenges with grace and ease.

Nutrition is a cornerstone of preventive health. The food we consume provides the building blocks for our cells and tissues, fuels our energy levels, and influences our mood and cognitive function. A balanced diet rich in whole, unprocessed foods, including fruits, vegetables, whole grains, and healthy fats, provides the nutrients necessary for optimal health and well-being. It supports the immune system, protects against chronic diseases, and promotes longevity. By making conscious choices about the foods we eat, we can nourish our bodies from the inside out and lay the groundwork for a vibrant and healthy life.

Physical activity is another essential component of preventive health. Regular exercise not only strengthens muscles and bones but also improves cardiovascular health, boosts metabolism, and reduces the risk of chronic diseases such as heart disease, diabetes, and certain types of cancer. It also has profound benefits for mental health, reducing stress, anxiety, and depression, and promoting a sense of well-being. Incorporating physical activity into our daily routines can be as simple as taking a brisk walk, going for a bike ride, or dancing to our favorite music. The key is to find activities that we enjoy and make them a regular part of our lives.

Stress management is a critical aspect of preventive health. Chronic stress can wreak havoc on our physical and mental health, suppressing the immune system, disrupting sleep patterns, and contributing to a host of health problems. Fortunately, there are many effective ways to manage stress, including mindfulness meditation, yoga, deep breathing exercises, and spending time in nature. By developing healthy coping mechanisms for stress, we can protect our health and well-being and cultivate a greater sense of inner peace.

Sleep is often overlooked but is essential for preventive health. During sleep, our bodies repair and restore themselves, consolidating memories, regulating hormones, and strengthening the immune system. Adequate sleep is crucial for cognitive function, emotional well-being, and physical health. By prioritizing sleep and establishing healthy sleep habits, such as maintaining a consistent sleep schedule, creating a relaxing bedtime routine, and avoiding caffeine and electronics before bed, we can optimize our health and well-being.

Beyond these core pillars of preventive health, there are many other wellness habits that can contribute to a long and healthy life. Maintaining a healthy weight, avoiding tobacco and excessive alcohol consumption, practicing safe sex, and getting regular checkups and screenings are all important preventive measures. Additionally, cultivating positive relationships, engaging in meaningful activities, and fostering a sense of purpose and connection can enhance our overall well-being and contribute to a fulfilling life.

Building lifelong wellness habits is not about striving for perfection but about making consistent choices that support our health and well-being. It is about recognizing that our health is a precious gift, and that by taking proactive steps to nurture it, we can create a life filled with vitality, joy, and purpose. By embracing preventive health and cultivating lifelong wellness habits, we can empower ourselves to live our best lives and create a brighter future for ourselves and our loved ones.

ppp

Sleep is not a luxury; it is a necessity. Just as the earth rests and renews itself each night, so too must we recharge our batteries through deep, restorative slumber.

SIX

NUTRITION: EATING FOR VIBRANT HEALTH.

The age-old adage "you are what you eat" holds profound truth, as the food we consume forms the very foundation of our physical, mental, and emotional well-being. Nutrition, the study of food and its impact on our bodies, is a cornerstone of vibrant health. The choices we make about what we put on our plates have a direct and lasting effect on our energy levels, mood, immune function, and overall vitality. By embracing a nourishing and balanced diet, we can unlock our body's innate potential for healing, vitality, and longevity.

At its core, nutrition is about providing our bodies with the essential nutrients they need to thrive. These nutrients include macronutrients such as carbohydrates, proteins, and fats, which provide energy and building blocks for cells and tissues. They also include micronutrients such as vitamins and minerals, which play crucial roles in various bodily functions, from immune system support to hormone regulation. A balanced diet that includes a variety of whole, unprocessed foods ensures that we receive the full spectrum of nutrients our bodies need to function optimally.

Fruits and vegetables are the superheroes of the nutritional world, packed with vitamins, minerals, fiber, and antioxidants. These vibrant foods protect against chronic diseases, reduce inflammation, and support healthy digestion. Aim to fill half of your plate with a colorful array of fruits and vegetables at each meal, choosing seasonal and locally sourced options whenever possible. Whole grains, such as brown rice, quinoa, and whole wheat bread, provide sustained energy, fiber, and essential nutrients. They are a far healthier alternative to refined grains, which have been stripped of their nutritional value.

Proteins are the building blocks of our bodies, essential for growth, repair, and maintenance of tissues. Choose lean protein sources such as fish, poultry, beans, lentils, and tofu. Healthy fats, found in avocados, nuts, seeds, and olive oil, are crucial for brain health, hormone balance, and cardiovascular health. Include these fats in moderation as part of a balanced diet. Limit processed foods, sugary drinks, and unhealthy fats, which can contribute to inflammation, weight gain, and chronic diseases.

Beyond simply providing essential nutrients, food has a profound impact on our energy levels and mood. Complex carbohydrates, such as those found in whole grains and legumes, provide sustained energy throughout the day, preventing the spikes and crashes associated with refined sugars. Protein-rich foods help to stabilize blood sugar levels and promote satiety, keeping us feeling fuller for longer. Healthy fats support brain function and mood regulation, while vitamins and minerals play crucial roles in neurotransmitter production and overall mental well-being.

The gut microbiome, a complex community of trillions of bacteria that reside in our digestive tract, also plays a crucial role in our health. These beneficial bacteria aid in digestion, nutrient absorption, immune function, and even mood regulation. A diet rich in fiber, found in fruits, vegetables, and whole grains, nourishes the gut microbiome and promotes a healthy balance of bacteria. Probiotic-rich foods, such as yogurt, kefir, and sauerkraut, can also support a healthy gut microbiome.

Eating for vibrant health is not about deprivation or strict diets but about making informed choices and nourishing our bodies with wholesome, delicious foods. It is about listening to our bodies' hunger and fullness cues, savoring each bite, and enjoying the social and cultural aspects of food. It is about recognizing that food is not merely fuel but a source of pleasure, nourishment, and connection.

By embracing a balanced and nourishing diet, we can unlock our body's innate potential for healing, vitality, and longevity. We can protect against chronic diseases, boost our immune system, enhance our mood and cognitive function, and cultivate a vibrant and thriving life. Eating for vibrant health is a lifelong journey, one that involves continuous learning, experimentation, and adaptation. It is a journey that is well worth taking, as the rewards are immeasurable.

ppp

Sunlight, the golden elixir of life, bathes us in its warmth and nourishes us with vital vitamin D. Embrace the sun's rays in moderation, and let its light illuminate your path to health and happiness.

SEVEN

Herbal Medicine: Nature's Gentle Remedies.

In the heart of nature's embrace lies a treasure trove of healing potential – the world of herbal medicine. For millennia, humans have turned to plants for their therapeutic properties, utilizing their leaves, roots, flowers, and seeds to alleviate ailments and promote well-being. Herbal medicine, a cornerstone of traditional healing systems across the globe, offers a gentle yet powerful approach to health and wellness, harnessing the innate wisdom of nature to restore balance and vitality.

The concept of herbal medicine is rooted in the understanding that plants contain a vast array of bioactive compounds, each with its unique therapeutic effects. These compounds, including alkaloids, flavonoids, tannins, and essential oils, interact with the body's complex systems to promote healing, reduce inflammation, boost immunity, and support overall health. Herbal remedies can be administered in various forms, including teas, tinctures, capsules, powders, and topical preparations, making them versatile and adaptable to individual needs.

One of the most appealing aspects of herbal medicine is its gentle nature. Unlike many pharmaceutical drugs, which often come with a long list of potential side effects, herbal remedies tend to be well-tolerated by the body. This is not to say that herbal remedies are without risk, as some can interact with medications or cause allergic reactions. However, when used responsibly and under the guidance of a qualified healthcare practitioner, herbal medicine can offer a safe and effective alternative or complement to conventional medicine.

The effectiveness of herbal medicine is supported by a growing body of scientific evidence. Numerous studies have demonstrated the therapeutic benefits of various herbs for a wide range of conditions. For example, chamomile has been shown to reduce anxiety and promote sleep, ginger to alleviate nausea and digestive discomfort, and echinacea to boost immune function. These are just a few examples of the many herbs that have been scientifically validated for their medicinal properties.

One of the unique strengths of herbal medicine lies in its holistic approach to health. Herbalists view the individual as a whole, recognizing the interconnectedness of mind, body, and spirit. Rather than simply targeting symptoms, herbal medicine seeks to address the root causes of illness, promoting overall balance and harmony within the body. This approach often involves lifestyle modifications, dietary changes, and other natural therapies in conjunction with herbal remedies.

Herbal medicine also emphasizes the importance of preventative care. By strengthening the body's natural defenses and promoting overall well-being, herbal remedies can help to prevent illness and disease. This proactive approach to health aligns with the growing recognition that true health is not merely the absence of disease but a state of vibrant vitality and well-being.

The world of herbal medicine is vast and diverse, with countless plants offering unique healing properties. Some of the most commonly used herbs include:

Chamomile: Known for its calming and sleep-promoting effects.

Ginger: Renowned for its ability to alleviate nausea, digestive discomfort, and inflammation.

Echinacea: A popular immune booster, often used to prevent and treat colds and flu.

Garlic: A potent antimicrobial and immune stimulant, with potential benefits for cardiovascular health.

Turmeric: A powerful anti-inflammatory spice, used for various conditions, including arthritis and pain.

This is just a small sampling of the many herbs that have been used for centuries to promote health and well-being.

As with any form of medicine, it is important to use herbal remedies responsibly and under the guidance of a qualified healthcare practitioner. Herbalists are trained in the safe and effective use of herbs, and can tailor treatment plans to individual needs and health conditions. By working with a qualified herbalist, you can harness the power of nature's gentle remedies to support your health and well-being.

In a world increasingly dominated by synthetic drugs and invasive procedures, herbal medicine offers a refreshing and holistic alternative. It is a testament to the enduring wisdom of nature, a reminder that the Earth provides us with everything we need to heal and thrive. By embracing the power of herbal medicine, we can tap into the innate healing potential of plants and embark on a journey toward vibrant health and well-being.

ೊೊೊ

Breathe in the fresh air, let it fill your lungs and revitalize your spirit. Clean air is a precious gift, essential for optimal health and well-being. Protect it, cherish it, and let it nourish your body from within.

EIGHT

HYDROTHERAPY: WATER'S HEALING POWER.

Water, the elixir of life, holds a profound ability to heal and rejuvenate the human body. This fundamental element, which constitutes a significant portion of our bodies and the Earth itself, has been revered for its therapeutic properties since ancient times. Hydrotherapy, the use of water in various forms and temperatures for healing purposes, harnesses this innate power to promote physical, mental, and emotional well-being.

The concept of hydrotherapy is rooted in the understanding that water has unique physical properties that can be manipulated to achieve specific therapeutic effects. These properties include temperature, pressure, buoyancy, and viscosity. By varying these factors, hydrotherapy can be tailored to address a wide range of health conditions, from chronic pain and inflammation to stress and anxiety.

One of the most fundamental principles of hydrotherapy is the use of temperature to influence physiological processes. Warm water, for example, can promote relaxation, increase blood flow, and reduce muscle tension. Hot water can further enhance these effects, while also stimulating the immune system and promoting detoxification. Cold water, on the other hand, can reduce inflammation, numb pain, and boost circulation. Alternating hot and cold water, known as contrast hydrotherapy, can further enhance these benefits by stimulating the lymphatic system and promoting detoxification.

The application of pressure is another key element of hydrotherapy. Water pressure can be used to massage muscles, improve circulation, and reduce swelling. This can be achieved through various methods, such as underwater massage, whirlpool baths, and hydrotherapy showers. The buoyancy of water, which reduces the impact of gravity on the body, can be particularly beneficial for individuals with joint pain or mobility issues. Water-based exercises, such as swimming and water aerobics, can provide a low-impact workout that strengthens muscles and improves cardiovascular health.

Hydrotherapy encompasses a wide range of techniques, each with its unique therapeutic benefits. Some of the most common hydrotherapy modalities include:

Baths: Warm baths can promote relaxation, reduce muscle tension, and improve sleep. Adding Epsom salts or essential oils can further enhance the therapeutic effects.

Showers: Alternating hot and cold showers can stimulate circulation, boost immunity, and invigorate the body.

Compresses: Warm or cold compresses can be applied to specific areas of the body to reduce pain, inflammation, and swelling.

Wraps: Wet wraps, such as those used in constitutional hydrotherapy, can promote detoxification, improve circulation, and support the immune system.

Immersion therapy: Soaking in a warm pool or hot tub can provide pain relief, relaxation, and improved range of motion.

Hydrotherapy has been shown to be effective for a wide range of health conditions, including:

Arthritis: Hydrotherapy can reduce pain, stiffness, and inflammation associated with arthritis.

Fibromyalgia: Warm water therapy can alleviate pain, fatigue, and sleep disturbances associated with fibromyalgia.

Chronic pain: Hydrotherapy can provide drug-free pain relief for various chronic pain conditions.

Stress and anxiety: Warm baths and relaxation techniques can reduce stress hormones and promote relaxation.

Sports injuries: Cold water therapy can reduce inflammation and swelling, while warm water therapy can promote healing and recovery.

While hydrotherapy is generally safe and well-tolerated, it is important to consult with a qualified healthcare practitioner before starting any hydrotherapy treatment, especially if you have any underlying health conditions. A qualified hydrotherapist can assess your individual needs and develop a personalized treatment plan that is safe and effective for you.

Incorporating hydrotherapy into your wellness routine can be a simple yet powerful way to enhance your health and well-being. Whether you enjoy a relaxing bath at home, take a dip in a hot tub, or participate in a guided hydrotherapy session, the healing power of water can provide a myriad of benefits for both body and mind. By embracing this ancient practice, you can tap into the restorative power of nature and unlock your body's innate capacity for healing and rejuvenation.

ϷϷϷ

Your heart is a garden, and your emotions are the seeds. Plant seeds of joy, gratitude, and love, and watch your heart blossom with health and vitality.

NINE

MIND-BODY CONNECTION: CULTIVATING INNER PEACE FOR OUTER HEALTH.

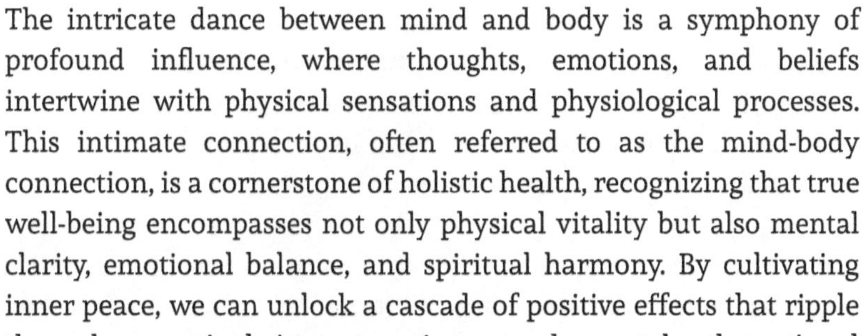

The intricate dance between mind and body is a symphony of profound influence, where thoughts, emotions, and beliefs intertwine with physical sensations and physiological processes. This intimate connection, often referred to as the mind-body connection, is a cornerstone of holistic health, recognizing that true well-being encompasses not only physical vitality but also mental clarity, emotional balance, and spiritual harmony. By cultivating inner peace, we can unlock a cascade of positive effects that ripple through our entire being, promoting not only mental and emotional well-being but also physical health and resilience.

The mind, a powerful instrument capable of both creation and destruction, wields a profound influence over our physical health.

Chronic stress, anxiety, and negative emotions can trigger a cascade of physiological responses, including the release of stress hormones such as cortisol and adrenaline. These hormones, while essential for survival in short bursts, can wreak havoc on our bodies when chronically elevated, suppressing the immune system, disrupting sleep patterns, and contributing to a host of health problems, from heart disease and diabetes to digestive disorders and autoimmune conditions.

Conversely, positive emotions such as joy, gratitude, and contentment can have a profound healing effect on the body. Studies have shown that positive emotions can boost the immune system, reduce inflammation, lower blood pressure, and even promote longevity. By cultivating a positive mindset and fostering emotional well-being, we create an internal environment conducive to healing and vitality.

The practice of mindfulness, a cornerstone of mind-body medicine, offers a powerful tool for cultivating inner peace and promoting overall health. Mindfulness involves paying non-judgmental attention to the present moment, observing our thoughts and emotions without getting caught up in them. This simple yet profound practice has been shown to reduce stress, anxiety, and depression, improve sleep quality, and enhance overall well-being. By cultivating mindfulness, we can develop a greater awareness of our thoughts and emotions, allowing us to respond to them in a more skillful and compassionate way.

Yoga, another powerful mind-body practice, combines physical postures, breathwork, and meditation to promote physical and mental well-being. The physical practice of yoga strengthens and stretches the body, improving flexibility, balance, and strength. The breathwork component of yoga helps to calm the nervous system, reduce stress, and promote relaxation. The meditative aspect of yoga cultivates mindfulness, self-awareness, and inner peace. By integrating these three elements, yoga offers a holistic approach to health and well-being, nurturing both the body and the mind.

In addition to mindfulness and yoga, there are many other practices that can help to cultivate inner peace and promote outer health. Spending time in nature, connecting with loved ones, engaging in creative pursuits, and practicing gratitude are just a few examples of activities that can nourish the soul and promote overall well-being. By incorporating these practices into our daily lives, we can create a foundation of inner peace that supports our physical, mental, and emotional health.

The mind-body connection is a dynamic and ever-evolving relationship. By cultivating inner peace, we can create a ripple effect that extends far beyond our own well-being. Our inner peace can radiate outward, influencing our relationships, our communities, and even the world around us. When we are at peace with ourselves, we are more likely to be compassionate, kind, and understanding towards others. We are more likely to create positive change in our lives and in the world.

By recognizing the profound interconnectedness of mind and body, we can unlock our innate capacity for healing, vitality, and well-being. By cultivating inner peace, we can create a life that is not only physically healthy but also mentally clear, emotionally balanced, and spiritually fulfilling. The journey toward inner peace is a lifelong endeavor, but the rewards are immeasurable. As we nurture our inner peace, we create a ripple effect of positive change that extends far beyond ourselves, touching the lives of those around us and contributing to a more peaceful and harmonious world.

In the pursuit of meaning and purpose, look to the wisdom of the ages. Explore your spiritual connection, embrace your unique gifts, and discover the path that leads to a life of fulfillment and joy.

TEN

DETOXIFICATION: CLEANSING FOR RENEWAL.

In our modern world, we are constantly exposed to a myriad of toxins, both from external sources and those generated within our own bodies. Environmental pollutants, processed foods, stress, and even our own metabolic processes can contribute to a buildup of toxins that can burden our organs and systems, leading to fatigue, sluggishness, and a host of health problems. Detoxification, the process of cleansing and purifying the body, offers a pathway to renewal, restoring vitality, balance, and optimal health.

At its core, detoxification is about supporting the body's natural processes of elimination and cleansing. Our bodies are equipped with sophisticated detoxification systems, including the liver, kidneys, lungs, skin, and lymphatic system. These organs and systems work tirelessly to filter, neutralize, and eliminate toxins from the body. However, in today's toxic world, these systems can become overburdened, leading to a buildup of toxins that can impair their function and compromise our health.

Detoxification aims to support and enhance these natural processes, providing the body with the tools it needs to efficiently eliminate toxins and restore balance. There are many different approaches to detoxification, ranging from simple dietary changes to more intensive cleansing programs. The most effective approach will vary depending on individual needs and health goals.

One of the most fundamental ways to support detoxification is through dietary modifications. A diet rich in whole, unprocessed foods, including fruits, vegetables, whole grains, and lean protein, provides the nutrients necessary for optimal detoxification. These foods are packed with vitamins, minerals, and antioxidants that support the liver, kidneys, and other organs involved in detoxification. Additionally, fiber-rich foods, such as fruits, vegetables, and legumes, promote healthy digestion and elimination, helping to remove waste and toxins from the body.

Certain foods and beverages can further enhance detoxification. Cruciferous vegetables, such as broccoli, cauliflower, and Brussels sprouts, contain compounds that support liver detoxification. Green tea is rich in antioxidants and has been shown to promote liver health. Lemon water, when consumed first thing in the morning, can stimulate digestion and help to flush out toxins.

In addition to dietary changes, there are many other natural therapies that can support detoxification. Herbal remedies, such as milk thistle, dandelion root, and burdock root, have been used for centuries to support liver function and promote detoxification. Hydrotherapy, the therapeutic use of water, can also be beneficial for detoxification. Saunas and steam baths, for example, can help to eliminate toxins through sweat, while Epsom salt baths can draw out toxins through the skin.

While detoxification can offer numerous benefits, it is important to approach it with caution and under the guidance of a qualified healthcare practitioner. Some detoxification programs can be quite intensive and may not be suitable for everyone, especially those with underlying health conditions. A qualified practitioner can help to assess your individual needs and develop a detoxification plan that is safe and effective for you.

The benefits of detoxification can be profound. By supporting the body's natural detoxification processes, we can:

Improve energy levels: Eliminating toxins can reduce fatigue and increase vitality.

Enhance mental clarity: Toxins can cloud the mind and impair cognitive function. Detoxification can promote mental clarity and focus.

Boost immune function: A clean and healthy body is better equipped to fight off infection and disease.

Improve digestion: Detoxification can support healthy digestion and elimination, reducing bloating, constipation, and other digestive problems.

Promote healthy skin: Toxins can contribute to skin problems such as acne, eczema, and psoriasis. Detoxification can improve skin health and radiance.

Reduce inflammation: Toxins can trigger inflammation throughout the body, contributing to various health problems. Detoxification can help to reduce inflammation and promote healing.

Detoxification is not a one-time event but an ongoing process. By incorporating healthy habits into our daily lives, such as eating a balanced diet, exercising regularly, managing stress, and getting enough sleep, we can support our body's natural detoxification processes and promote optimal health and well-being.

While the concept of detoxification may seem trendy or new age, it is actually a practice that has been around for centuries. Many traditional healing systems, such as Ayurveda and Traditional Chinese Medicine, place great emphasis on detoxification as a fundamental aspect of health and well-being. By embracing the wisdom of these ancient traditions and combining it with modern scientific knowledge, we can harness the power of detoxification to cleanse, renew, and revitalize our bodies.

ᗡᗡᗡ

We are not isolated beings but interconnected threads in the vast tapestry of life. Build supportive relationships, foster a sense of community, and let the power of connection uplift and empower you.

ELEVEN
Stress Management: Finding Balance in a Busy World.

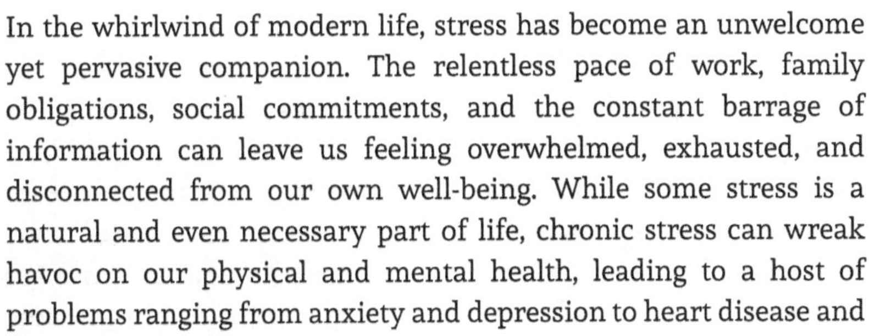

In the whirlwind of modern life, stress has become an unwelcome yet pervasive companion. The relentless pace of work, family obligations, social commitments, and the constant barrage of information can leave us feeling overwhelmed, exhausted, and disconnected from our own well-being. While some stress is a natural and even necessary part of life, chronic stress can wreak havoc on our physical and mental health, leading to a host of problems ranging from anxiety and depression to heart disease and immune dysfunction.

Fortunately, there are many effective strategies for managing stress and finding balance in our busy lives. These strategies encompass a holistic approach that addresses not only the symptoms of stress but also the underlying causes. By incorporating these practices into our daily routines, we can cultivate resilience, enhance our well-being, and create a more peaceful and fulfilling life.

One of the most fundamental stress management techniques is mindfulness. This ancient practice involves paying non-judgmental attention to the present moment, observing our thoughts and emotions without getting caught up in them. Mindfulness can be practiced through meditation, yoga, or simply by taking a few moments each day to focus on our breath and tune into our senses. By cultivating mindfulness, we can develop a greater awareness of our stress triggers, learn to respond to them in a more skillful way, and create a sense of inner calm amidst the chaos of daily life.

Another powerful tool for stress management is physical activity. Exercise has been shown to have numerous benefits for both physical and mental health. It releases endorphins, natural mood boosters that can help to reduce stress, anxiety, and depression. Exercise also helps to improve sleep quality, boost energy levels, and strengthen the immune system. Finding an activity that you enjoy, whether it's walking, running, swimming, dancing, or yoga, can make exercise a sustainable and enjoyable part of your daily routine.

In addition to mindfulness and exercise, there are many other stress management techniques that can be effective. Deep breathing exercises, such as diaphragmatic breathing or alternate nostril breathing, can help to calm the nervous system and reduce stress hormones. Progressive muscle relaxation, a technique that involves tensing and relaxing different muscle groups, can also promote relaxation and reduce muscle tension.

Maintaining a healthy lifestyle is also crucial for stress management. Eating a balanced diet, getting enough sleep, and avoiding excessive caffeine and alcohol can all contribute to a more resilient and stress-resistant body and mind. Connecting with loved ones, spending time in nature, and engaging in activities that bring joy and fulfillment can also help to reduce stress and promote overall well-being.

It is important to recognize that stress management is not a one-size-fits-all approach. What works for one person may not work for another. It is important to experiment with different techniques and find what works best for you. If you are struggling to manage stress on your own, it is important to seek professional help. A therapist or counselor can provide guidance and support in developing effective stress management strategies.

In our fast-paced world, it is easy to get caught up in the daily grind and neglect our own well-being. However, by prioritizing stress management and incorporating these practices into our lives, we can cultivate resilience, enhance our health, and create a more balanced and fulfilling life. Stress may be an inevitable part of life, but it doesn't have to control us. By taking proactive steps to manage stress, we can reclaim our power, find inner peace, and thrive in the face of life's challenges.

ᗡᗡᗡ

*Live in harmony with the earth, for it is our home,
our sustainer, our teacher. Embrace sustainable
living, reduce your ecological footprint, and let your
actions reflect your love for the planet.*

TWELVE

EXERCISE: MOVING FOR JOY AND VITALITY.

In the tapestry of human existence, movement is not merely a means of transportation but a fundamental expression of life itself. From the rhythmic beating of our hearts to the subtle movements of our breath, our bodies are designed for motion. Exercise, the intentional engagement in physical activity, harnesses this innate potential, offering a pathway to not only physical health but also mental clarity, emotional balance, and a profound sense of joy and vitality.

The benefits of exercise are far-reaching and encompass virtually every aspect of our being. Physically, exercise strengthens muscles and bones, improves cardiovascular health, boosts metabolism, and helps to maintain a healthy weight. It can reduce the risk of chronic diseases such as heart disease, stroke, type 2 diabetes, and certain types of cancer. Exercise also enhances flexibility, balance, and coordination, reducing the risk of falls and injuries.

Beyond its physical benefits, exercise has a profound impact on our mental and emotional well-being. It stimulates the release of endorphins, natural mood boosters that can alleviate stress, anxiety, and depression. Exercise also promotes the growth of new brain cells and enhances cognitive function, improving memory, focus, and creativity. It can even help to prevent age-related cognitive decline.

The joy of movement is a fundamental human experience. From the exuberance of a child at play to the graceful movements of a dancer, the act of moving our bodies can bring immense pleasure and satisfaction. Exercise can be a source of fun, connection, and self-expression. Whether it's dancing to our favorite music, hiking in nature, or playing a sport with friends, engaging in physical activity that we enjoy can make exercise a sustainable and rewarding part of our lives.

Finding joy in movement is key to making exercise a lifelong habit. Rather than viewing exercise as a chore or a punishment, we can approach it with a sense of playfulness and curiosity. Experimenting with different activities, setting realistic goals, and celebrating our successes can help to make exercise a positive and enjoyable experience. It's also important to listen to our bodies and choose activities that feel good and are appropriate for our fitness level.

Incorporating exercise into our daily routines doesn't have to be complicated or time-consuming. Even small amounts of physical activity can have significant benefits. Taking a brisk walk during your lunch break, doing a few stretches in the morning, or dancing in your living room for a few minutes can all contribute to your overall health and well-being. The key is to find ways to make movement a natural and enjoyable part of your day.

Exercise is not just about achieving a certain body shape or size. It's about cultivating a sense of vitality, strength, and resilience.

It's about connecting with our bodies and honoring their innate capacity for movement. It's about finding joy and fulfillment in the act of moving. By embracing exercise as a celebration of life, we can unlock its full potential to transform our health and well-being.

The journey to a more active lifestyle is a personal one. There is no one-size-fits-all approach. The most important thing is to find activities that you enjoy and that fit into your lifestyle. By listening to your body, setting realistic goals, and celebrating your successes, you can create a sustainable exercise routine that brings you joy, vitality, and a renewed sense of well-being.

ᑭᑭᑭ

The naturopathic doctor is not merely a practitioner but a guide, a teacher, and a partner in your journey toward health and well-being. Trust their wisdom, embrace their guidance, and together, you can unlock the full potential of your body's innate healing power.

THIRTEEN

SLEEP: RECHARGING YOUR BODY'S BATTERIES.

In the tapestry of life, sleep is the golden thread that weaves together our physical, mental, and emotional well-being. It is the restorative balm that soothes our weary souls, the silent healer that mends our bodies, and the essential recharge that powers our minds. Sleep, often underestimated and undervalued in our fast-paced world, is not merely a passive state of rest but an active process of renewal and rejuvenation.

During sleep, our bodies embark on a remarkable journey of restoration and repair. Cells regenerate, muscles rebuild, and energy stores are replenished. The immune system strengthens its defenses, preparing to fight off infection and disease. Hormones are balanced, regulating everything from appetite and metabolism to stress response and mood. The brain, the command center of our being, consolidates memories, processes information, and prepares for the challenges of the day ahead.

Sleep deprivation, on the other hand, can have devastating

consequences for our health and well-being. Lack of sleep can impair cognitive function, leading to difficulty concentrating, making decisions, and remembering information. It can also affect our mood, increasing irritability, anxiety, and depression. Chronic sleep deprivation has been linked to a host of health problems, including obesity, diabetes, heart disease, and stroke. It can even weaken the immune system, making us more susceptible to illness.

The importance of sleep cannot be overstated. It is not a luxury but a necessity, a fundamental pillar of health and well-being. By prioritizing sleep and establishing healthy sleep habits, we can optimize our physical and mental performance, enhance our mood, and protect ourselves from a wide range of health problems.

Creating a sleep-conducive environment is essential for quality rest. This includes keeping your bedroom cool, dark, and quiet. Investing in a comfortable mattress and pillows can also make a significant difference. Establishing a regular sleep schedule, going to bed and waking up at the same time each day, can help to regulate your body's natural sleep-wake cycle.

Avoiding caffeine and alcohol before bed is also important, as these substances can interfere with sleep. Creating a relaxing bedtime routine, such as taking a warm bath, reading a book, or listening to calming music, can help to signal to your body that it's time to wind down and prepare for sleep. Limiting exposure to electronic devices before bed is also crucial, as the blue light emitted from these devices can suppress the production of melatonin, a hormone that regulates sleep.

If you are struggling with sleep problems, it is important to seek help from a qualified healthcare provider. There are many effective treatments for sleep disorders, ranging from lifestyle changes and relaxation techniques to medication and therapy.

Sleep is not merely a time for rest, it is a time for renewal, rejuvenation, and revitalization. It is a time for our bodies and minds to heal and restore themselves, preparing us for the challenges and opportunities of the day ahead. By prioritizing sleep and establishing healthy sleep habits, we can unlock our full potential for health, happiness, and well-being.

ᐯᐯᐯ

Every step you take, every breath you breathe, every choice you make is an opportunity to nurture your health and well-being. Embrace the healing touch of nature, and let it guide you toward a life of vitality, joy, and fulfillment.

FOURTEEN

SUNLIGHT: SOAKING UP NATURE'S VITAMIN D.

Sunlight, often hailed as the lifeblood of our planet, is also a vital source of nourishment for the human body. Beyond its warmth and illuminating power, sunlight offers a treasure trove of health benefits, most notably the production of vitamin D, a crucial nutrient for our overall well-being. The act of basking in the sun's rays, a simple yet profound pleasure, is not merely an indulgence but a fundamental act of self-care that nourishes our bodies from the inside out.

Vitamin D, often referred to as the "sunshine vitamin," is a fat-soluble vitamin that plays a pivotal role in numerous bodily functions. It is essential for calcium absorption, bone health, immune function, and cellular growth. Vitamin D receptors are found throughout the body, suggesting that its influence extends far beyond its well-known role in bone health. Research has linked vitamin D deficiency to a wide range of health problems, including osteoporosis, autoimmune diseases, cardiovascular disease, and even certain types of cancer.

While some vitamin D can be obtained through diet, such as fatty fish, egg yolks, and fortified foods, the most efficient way to obtain this essential nutrient is through sun exposure. When sunlight strikes our skin, it triggers a chemical reaction that converts a cholesterol-like substance into vitamin D3, the active form of vitamin D. The amount of vitamin D produced depends on various factors, including the intensity of sunlight, skin tone, and duration of exposure.

The benefits of vitamin D are numerous and far-reaching. It plays a crucial role in maintaining strong bones and teeth by promoting calcium absorption and regulating bone metabolism. Vitamin D also supports immune function by enhancing the activity of immune cells and reducing inflammation. It has been shown to reduce the risk of autoimmune diseases, such as multiple sclerosis and rheumatoid arthritis.

Vitamin D also has a significant impact on mental health. It plays a role in regulating mood and has been linked to a reduced risk of depression and seasonal affective disorder (SAD). Studies have also suggested that vitamin D may play a role in cognitive function and memory.

Despite its importance, vitamin D deficiency is a widespread problem. Factors such as limited sun exposure, use of sunscreen, darker skin pigmentation, and certain medical conditions can all contribute to low levels of vitamin D. The elderly and those living in northern latitudes are particularly at risk.

Fortunately, there are simple and effective ways to ensure adequate vitamin D levels. Spending time outdoors in the sunshine is the most natural and enjoyable way to boost your vitamin D levels. Aim for 15-20 minutes of sun exposure on your arms and legs several times a week, without sunscreen, during the hours when the sun's rays are most intense. If you have darker skin or live in a northern climate, you may need more sun exposure or consider taking a vitamin D supplement.

While sun exposure is essential for vitamin D production, it's important to balance the benefits with the risks. Excessive sun exposure can increase the risk of skin cancer, so it's important to take precautions such as wearing protective clothing and using sunscreen when spending extended periods in the sun.

Incorporating vitamin D-rich foods into your diet can also help to ensure adequate levels. Fatty fish, such as salmon, tuna, and mackerel, are excellent sources of vitamin D. Egg yolks, fortified dairy products, and mushrooms exposed to ultraviolet light are also good options.

If you are concerned about your vitamin D levels, talk to your healthcare provider. They can recommend a blood test to check your levels and advise you on the best way to ensure you are getting enough of this essential nutrient.

Sunlight, the life-giving force of nature, offers us a precious gift in the form of vitamin D. By soaking up the sun's rays in moderation and incorporating vitamin D-rich foods into our diet, we can nourish our bodies, strengthen our bones, boost our immune system, and enhance our overall well-being.

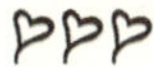

The path to health is not a linear one but a winding road with twists and turns. Be patient, be kind to yourself, and trust in the wisdom of your body to guide you toward healing and wholeness.

FIFTEEN

AIR QUALITY: BREATHING FOR OPTIMAL HEALTH.

The simple act of breathing, often taken for granted, is the most fundamental and essential function of the human body. With each inhale, we draw in the life-giving oxygen that fuels our cells, nourishes our tissues, and sustains our very existence. The quality of the air we breathe, however, plays a critical role in our overall health and well-being. In an era of increasing pollution and environmental degradation, the importance of clean air for optimal health cannot be overstated.

Air quality refers to the degree to which the air is free from pollutants and contaminants that can harm human health and the environment. These pollutants can come from a variety of sources, including industrial emissions, vehicle exhaust, agricultural practices, and natural events such as wildfires. The most common air pollutants include particulate matter (tiny particles that can lodge in the lungs), ground-level ozone, carbon monoxide, sulfur dioxide, and nitrogen dioxide. These pollutants can cause a wide range of health problems, from respiratory irritation and breathing difficulties to cardiovascular disease and cancer.

The respiratory system is particularly vulnerable to the effects of air pollution. When we breathe in polluted air, these harmful substances can irritate and inflame the airways, leading to coughing, wheezing, and shortness of breath. Over time, exposure to air pollution can damage the lungs and increase the risk of respiratory diseases such as asthma, bronchitis, and emphysema.

Air pollution can also have a significant impact on cardiovascular health. Studies have shown that exposure to air pollution can increase the risk of heart attack, stroke, and other cardiovascular events. This is because air pollution can damage blood vessels, increase inflammation, and disrupt the normal functioning of the heart.

The effects of air pollution are not limited to the respiratory and cardiovascular systems. Air pollution can also affect the nervous system, immune system, and endocrine system. It has been linked to a variety of health problems, including neurological disorders, cancer, and reproductive problems.

While air pollution is a global problem, there are steps we can take to protect ourselves and our loved ones from its harmful effects. One of the most important things we can do is to be aware of the air quality in our communities and take steps to reduce our exposure when air pollution levels are high. This may involve staying indoors, avoiding strenuous outdoor activities, and using air purifiers.

Making choices that support clean air can also have a significant impact. Choosing public transportation, walking, biking, or carpooling instead of driving alone can reduce vehicle emissions. Supporting policies that promote clean energy and reduce industrial pollution can also help to improve air quality.

On an individual level, there are many things we can do to improve the air quality in our homes and workplaces. Using natural cleaning products, avoiding harsh chemicals, and ventilating our homes regularly can all help to reduce indoor air pollution. Planting trees and other vegetation can also help to purify the air and create a healthier environment.

Breathing clean air is essential for optimal health. By taking steps to reduce our exposure to air pollution and support clean air initiatives, we can protect ourselves and our loved ones from the harmful effects of this pervasive problem. Breathing clean air is not only a right, it is a necessity for a healthy and fulfilling life.

*Let food be thy medicine, and medicine be thy food.
Nourish your body with wholesome, unprocessed
foods that fuel your vitality and support your
body's natural healing processes.*

SIXTEEN

EMOTIONAL WELL-BEING: NURTURING A HEALTHY HEART.

The heart, often symbolized as the seat of emotions, is not merely a physical organ but a profound reflection of our inner world. Emotional well-being, a state of psychological and emotional health, plays a pivotal role in nurturing a healthy heart, both figuratively and literally. Our emotions, whether joy, sadness, anger, or fear, have a direct impact on our cardiovascular system, influencing heart rate, blood pressure, and even the risk of developing heart disease. By cultivating emotional well-being, we not only enhance our quality of life but also protect our hearts from the detrimental effects of stress, negativity, and emotional turmoil.

The link between emotional well-being and heart health is well-established. Chronic stress, anxiety, and depression have been linked to an increased risk of heart disease, stroke, and other cardiovascular problems. These negative emotions trigger a cascade of physiological responses, including the release of stress hormones such as cortisol and adrenaline, which can raise blood pressure, increase heart rate, and contribute to inflammation. Over time, these physiological changes can damage blood vessels, weaken the heart muscle, and increase the risk of cardiovascular disease.

Conversely, positive emotions such as joy, gratitude, and contentment have a protective effect on the heart. These emotions promote relaxation, reduce stress hormones, and improve cardiovascular function. Studies have shown that individuals who experience positive emotions regularly have lower blood pressure, reduced risk of heart disease, and even increased longevity.

Nurturing emotional well-being involves a multi-faceted approach that addresses both the mind and the body. One of the most effective ways to cultivate emotional well-being is through mindfulness practices. Mindfulness involves paying non-judgmental attention to the present moment, observing our thoughts and emotions without getting caught up in them. This simple yet profound practice has been shown to reduce stress, anxiety, and depression, improve mood, and enhance overall well-being.

Regular exercise is another powerful tool for nurturing emotional well-being. Physical activity releases endorphins, natural mood boosters that can alleviate stress, anxiety, and depression. Exercise also improves sleep quality, reduces fatigue, and enhances self-esteem, all of which contribute to emotional well-being.

Maintaining a healthy lifestyle is also crucial for emotional well-being. A balanced diet rich in whole, unprocessed foods provides the nutrients necessary for optimal brain function and mood regulation. Adequate sleep is essential for emotional balance, as sleep deprivation can exacerbate stress, anxiety, and depression. Avoiding excessive alcohol consumption and refraining from smoking are also important for emotional and physical health.

Social connection plays a vital role in emotional well-being. Strong relationships with friends, family, and community provide a sense of belonging, support, and purpose. Spending time with loved ones, engaging in meaningful conversations, and participating in social activities can all contribute to emotional well-being.

For those struggling with emotional difficulties, seeking professional help is crucial. Therapists and counselors can provide guidance and support in developing coping mechanisms, managing stress, and cultivating emotional well-being. Therapy can be an invaluable tool for individuals dealing with anxiety, depression, trauma, or other emotional challenges.

Nurturing emotional well-being is a lifelong journey that requires ongoing effort and commitment. It is about making conscious choices that prioritize our mental and emotional health, just as we prioritize our physical health. By cultivating positive emotions, managing stress effectively, and seeking support when needed, we can create a foundation of emotional well-being that nourishes our hearts and supports our overall health and happiness.

The heart, the wellspring of our emotions, deserves our utmost care and attention. By nurturing emotional well-being, we not only protect our hearts from the detrimental effects of stress and negativity but also unlock a cascade of positive effects that ripple through our entire being. A healthy heart is not just a physical organ but a reflection of a life lived with joy, gratitude, and love.

ϷϷϷ

Movement is life. Embrace physical activity as a celebration of your body's innate capacity for movement. Find joy in the simple act of moving, and let it invigorate your body and uplift your spirit.

SEVENTEEN

SPIRITUAL CONNECTION: FINDING MEANING AND PURPOSE.

In the depths of the human spirit lies a yearning for something greater than ourselves, a longing for connection, meaning, and purpose. This inherent desire for spiritual fulfillment is a fundamental aspect of human nature, transcending the boundaries of culture, religion, and individual beliefs. The pursuit of a spiritual connection is a deeply personal journey, one that involves exploring our inner landscape, seeking answers to life's big questions, and discovering a sense of purpose and meaning that resonates with our core values and beliefs.

Spirituality is a multifaceted concept that encompasses a wide range of beliefs, practices, and experiences. For some, spirituality may involve connecting with a higher power or divine being, while for others, it may simply be a sense of awe and wonder at the beauty and complexity of the natural world. Regardless of individual beliefs, the pursuit of a spiritual connection can offer a myriad of benefits for our overall well-being.

Research has shown that individuals who report a strong sense of spirituality tend to experience greater life satisfaction, resilience in the face of adversity, and a deeper sense of purpose and meaning. They also report lower levels of stress, anxiety, and depression, as well as improved physical health outcomes. This suggests that spirituality can play a significant role in our overall well-being, enhancing our mental, emotional, and physical health.

Finding a spiritual connection is a deeply personal journey, and there is no one-size-fits-all approach. Some individuals may find solace and meaning in organized religion, while others may prefer a more independent path. Some may connect with nature, while others may find inspiration in art, music, or literature. The key is to explore different avenues and discover what resonates most deeply with your own values and beliefs.

One of the most fundamental ways to cultivate a spiritual connection is through mindfulness practices. Mindfulness involves paying non-judgmental attention to the present moment, observing our thoughts, emotions, and sensations without getting caught up in them. This practice can help us to quiet the mind, connect with our inner wisdom, and cultivate a deeper sense of awareness and presence.

Another powerful way to connect with our spirituality is through spending time in nature. Nature has a way of grounding us, reminding us of our interconnectedness with the world around us, and inspiring a sense of awe and wonder. Whether it's a walk in the woods, a swim in the ocean, or simply gazing at the stars, spending time in nature can be a deeply spiritual experience.

Engaging in creative pursuits can also be a powerful way to connect with our spirituality. Whether it's painting, writing, music, or dance, creative expression allows us to tap into our inner world, express our emotions, and connect with something larger than ourselves.

The pursuit of a spiritual connection is not about achieving perfection or adhering to rigid dogma. It is about exploring our inner landscape, discovering our own unique path, and finding meaning and purpose in our lives. It is about connecting with something larger than ourselves, whether it's a higher power, the natural world, or our own inner wisdom. By embracing our spirituality, we can tap into a source of strength, resilience, and inspiration that can guide us through life's challenges and lead us toward a more fulfilling and meaningful existence.

ppp

Stress is a thief that steals our joy and vitality. Arm yourself with mindfulness, relaxation techniques, and healthy coping mechanisms to reclaim your peace and serenity.

EIGHTEEN

COMMUNITY: BUILDING SUPPORTIVE RELATIONSHIPS.

The human experience is fundamentally intertwined with the bonds we forge with others. We are social creatures, wired for connection, belonging, and mutual support. Community, the intricate web of relationships we weave with those around us, is a cornerstone of human well-being, offering a haven of support, encouragement, and shared experiences. Building supportive relationships within our communities is not merely a social nicety but a vital component of our overall health and happiness.

The power of community lies in its ability to provide a sense of belonging and connection. In a world that can often feel isolating and overwhelming, having a network of supportive individuals can make all the difference. Whether it's family, friends, neighbors, or colleagues, these connections offer a sense of security, acceptance, and understanding. They provide a safe space where we can share our joys and sorrows, celebrate our successes, and find solace in times of need.

Supportive relationships are not just about emotional support; they also have a profound impact on our physical and mental health. Studies have shown that individuals with strong social connections tend to live longer, healthier lives. They are less likely to experience stress, anxiety, and depression, and they have a stronger immune system and a lower risk of chronic diseases. The simple act of connecting with others can trigger the release of oxytocin, a hormone that promotes bonding, trust, and well-being.

Building supportive relationships takes time, effort, and intentionality. It involves stepping outside of our comfort zones, reaching out to others, and being willing to be vulnerable and open. It also requires us to be supportive and encouraging in return, offering a listening ear, a helping hand, or a shoulder to lean on when needed.

One of the most effective ways to build supportive relationships is through shared experiences. Whether it's volunteering for a cause we care about, joining a club or group that aligns with our interests, or simply spending time with friends and family, shared experiences create a sense of camaraderie and connection. They provide opportunities to learn from each other, support each other, and build lasting bonds.

Another important aspect of building supportive relationships is communication. Effective communication involves not only expressing our own needs and feelings but also actively listening to and understanding the needs and feelings of others. It involves being respectful, empathetic, and compassionate, even when we disagree. By communicating openly and honestly, we can build trust, deepen our connections, and create a safe space for vulnerability and growth.

In today's digital age, it's easy to become isolated and disconnected, even when surrounded by people. While technology can be a useful tool for staying connected, it's important to prioritize face-to-face interactions and meaningful conversations. Make time to meet up with friends and family, have lunch with a colleague, or simply chat with your neighbor. These small interactions can make a big difference in strengthening our connections and fostering a sense of community.

Building supportive relationships is an investment in our own well-being. By nurturing our connections with others, we create a network of support that can help us navigate life's challenges, celebrate our successes, and find meaning and purpose in our lives. The power of community is undeniable, and by investing in our relationships, we can create a life that is richer, more fulfilling, and more connected.

ᐅᐅᐅ

Water, the elixir of life, cleanses, refreshes, and revitalizes. Embrace the healing power of water, whether it's a warm bath, a cool shower, or a dip in the ocean.

NINETEEN

SUSTAINABLE LIVING: CARING FOR OUR PLANET AND OURSELVES.

In an era marked by environmental challenges and a growing awareness of our impact on the planet, sustainable living emerges as a beacon of hope, a pathway towards a harmonious coexistence with nature. It is a lifestyle choice that embraces the interconnectedness of all living beings, recognizing that our actions have consequences for both the environment and ourselves. By adopting sustainable practices, we not only safeguard the health of our planet but also nurture our own well-being, creating a more balanced and fulfilling life.

At its core, sustainable living is about making conscious choices that minimize our ecological footprint. It involves re-evaluating our consumption patterns, embracing mindful consumption, and prioritizing practices that conserve resources, reduce waste, and protect the environment. From the food we eat to the products we buy, the energy we use, and the waste we generate, every choice we make has an impact on the world around us.

One of the fundamental principles of sustainable living is reducing our consumption of resources. This includes minimizing our use of water, energy, and other natural resources. By taking shorter showers, turning off lights when we leave a room, and choosing energy-efficient appliances, we can significantly reduce our energy consumption and carbon footprint. Similarly, by reducing our water usage, fixing leaks, and collecting rainwater, we can conserve this precious resource and reduce our impact on the environment.

Another key aspect of sustainable living is reducing waste. This involves minimizing the amount of waste we generate in the first place, as well as finding ways to reuse, recycle, or compost the waste we do produce. By choosing products with minimal packaging, avoiding single-use plastics, and composting food scraps, we can significantly reduce the amount of waste that ends up in landfills, polluting our environment and contributing to climate change.

Sustainable living also encompasses mindful consumption. This means considering the environmental and social impact of our purchases and choosing products that are ethically sourced, produced using sustainable practices, and have minimal impact on the environment. It also means buying only what we need, avoiding impulse purchases, and investing in quality items that will last.

In addition to reducing our environmental impact, sustainable living also involves making choices that support our own health and well-being. This includes eating a balanced diet of whole, unprocessed foods, getting regular exercise, managing stress, and prioritizing sleep. It also involves cultivating a sense of gratitude, mindfulness, and connection with the natural world. By taking care of ourselves, we are better equipped to care for our planet.

Sustainable living is not about sacrificing comfort or convenience;

it's about finding creative and innovative ways to live in harmony with nature. It's about embracing simple pleasures, such as spending time outdoors, connecting with loved ones, and appreciating the beauty of the world around us. It's about finding joy in sustainable practices, such as growing our own food, supporting local farmers, and reducing our reliance on fossil fuels.

Sustainable living is a journey, not a destination. It's about making small changes that add up over time. It's about educating ourselves about the environmental and social impacts of our choices and making informed decisions that align with our values. It's about being mindful of our impact on the planet and taking responsibility for our actions.

By embracing sustainable living, we not only protect the health of our planet but also nurture our own well-being. We create a more balanced, fulfilling, and connected life. We become part of a movement that is shaping a brighter future for ourselves, our children, and generations to come. Sustainable living is not just a choice; it's a responsibility and an opportunity to create a more sustainable, equitable, and thriving world for all.

Open your heart to the healing power of nature. Let its beauty inspire you, its rhythms soothe you, and its wisdom guide you toward a life of vibrant health and well-being.

TWENTY

Naturopathic Doctor: Your Partner in Natural Health.

In the pursuit of holistic well-being, a naturopathic doctor emerges as a unique and invaluable partner. Distinct from conventional medical doctors, naturopathic doctors (NDs) offer a comprehensive approach to health that encompasses not only the physical body but also the mental, emotional, and spiritual aspects of an individual. Rooted in the principles of natural medicine, NDs strive to identify and address the root causes of disease, empower patients to take an active role in their health, and facilitate the body's innate ability to heal itself.

The foundation of naturopathic medicine lies in six core principles:

The Healing Power of Nature (Vis Medicatrix Naturae): NDs believe in the body's inherent wisdom to heal itself given the right conditions. They work to identify and remove obstacles to healing, allowing the body's natural processes to restore balance and health.

Identify and Treat the Cause (Tolle Causam): NDs focus on identifying and addressing the underlying causes of disease, rather than simply suppressing symptoms. They recognize that symptoms are often the body's way of signaling an imbalance, and they strive to restore balance by addressing the root of the problem.

First Do No Harm (Primum Non Nocere): NDs prioritize safe and gentle therapies that work in harmony with the body's natural processes. They avoid invasive procedures and harsh medications whenever possible, opting for natural remedies and lifestyle modifications that support the body's innate healing abilities.

Doctor as Teacher (Docere): NDs view themselves as educators, empowering patients to take an active role in their health and well-being. They provide information and guidance on nutrition, exercise, stress management, and other lifestyle factors that can promote optimal health.

Treat the Whole Person: NDs recognize that health is not just the absence of disease but a state of complete physical, mental, emotional, and spiritual well-being. They take a holistic approach to care, addressing all aspects of a person's life to promote optimal health and vitality.

Prevention: NDs emphasize the importance of prevention, working with patients to identify and address potential health risks before they become problematic. They focus on lifestyle modifications, such as diet, exercise, and stress management, that can help to prevent disease and promote long-term health.

Naturopathic doctors undergo rigorous training and education, including a four-year graduate-level naturopathic medical program. Their curriculum encompasses a wide range of subjects, including basic sciences, diagnostics, natural therapies, nutrition, and counseling. Upon graduation, NDs are required to pass a comprehensive licensing exam before they can practice.

NDs utilize a variety of natural therapies to support health and well-being. These therapies may include:

Clinical Nutrition: NDs provide personalized dietary recommendations based on individual needs and health goals. They may also recommend specific supplements to address nutrient deficiencies or support specific health conditions.

Botanical Medicine: NDs use plant-based remedies to support various bodily functions, alleviate symptoms, and promote healing.

Homeopathy: This gentle therapy utilizes highly diluted substances to stimulate the body's innate healing response.

Physical Medicine: This encompasses a variety of manual therapies, such as massage, manipulation, and hydrotherapy, to promote physical health and well-being.

Counseling: NDs provide guidance and support on stress management, lifestyle modifications, and other factors that can influence health and well-being.

Choosing a naturopathic doctor is a personal decision. It is important to find a practitioner who is licensed and experienced in treating your specific health concerns. By working collaboratively with a naturopathic doctor, you can develop a personalized health plan that empowers you to take charge of your health and achieve optimal well-being.

The benefits of working with a naturopathic doctor are numerous. NDs offer a safe, effective, and holistic approach to health that addresses the root causes of disease and empowers patients to take an active role in their own healing. By partnering with a naturopathic doctor, you can tap into the wisdom of nature and unlock your body's innate capacity for health and vitality.

ᛈᛈᛈ

In every challenge lies an opportunity for growth. Embrace the lessons that life offers you, and let them transform you into the healthiest, happiest version of yourself.

TWENTY-ONE
SUMMARY

The Healing Touch of Nature: Embracing Naturopathy for a Vibrant Life

In the tapestry of life, health is not merely the absence of disease but a vibrant symphony of interconnected elements. Naturopathy, a holistic system of medicine, recognizes this interconnectedness and seeks to nurture the body's innate wisdom for healing. By harnessing nature's medicine chest, embracing a holistic approach to health, and cultivating lifelong wellness habits, we can unlock our full potential for vitality, joy, and well-being.

At its core, naturopathy acknowledges the body's inherent intelligence, a vital force that guides its healing processes. This vital force is nourished and strengthened through a balanced and nourishing diet, the use of natural remedies, and the cultivation of a healthy mind-body connection. By prioritizing prevention and adopting sustainable lifestyle choices, we can empower ourselves to take charge of our health and create a life that is both vibrant and sustainable.

Nutrition plays a pivotal role in naturopathic medicine. By eating for vibrant health, we provide our bodies with the essential nutrients they need to thrive. A balanced diet rich in whole, unprocessed foods, including fruits, vegetables, whole grains, and healthy fats, supports optimal physical and mental function, strengthens the immune system, and protects against chronic diseases. By making conscious choices about the food we eat, we can nourish our bodies from the inside out and lay the groundwork for a healthy and fulfilling life.

Natural remedies, derived from plants, minerals, and other natural sources, offer a gentle yet powerful approach to healing. Herbal medicine, essential oils, probiotics, and other natural remedies can be used to support various bodily functions, alleviate symptoms, and promote overall well-being. By harnessing the wisdom of nature, we can tap into the healing potential of the earth and support our bodies' innate ability to heal themselves.

Holistic health recognizes the interconnectedness of mind, body, and spirit. By cultivating inner peace through mindfulness practices, yoga, and other stress-reducing techniques, we can create a harmonious internal environment that supports physical and emotional well-being. Stress, a major contributor to many health problems, can be effectively managed through a combination of lifestyle modifications, relaxation techniques, and natural remedies.

The importance of sleep cannot be overstated. Sleep is the time when our bodies repair and restore themselves, consolidating memories, regulating hormones, and strengthening the immune system. By prioritizing sleep and establishing healthy sleep habits, we can recharge our batteries, enhance our cognitive function, and improve our overall well-being.

Sunlight, a source of vital vitamin D, plays a crucial role in bone health, immune function, and mood regulation. By soaking up the sun's rays in moderation, we can reap the many benefits of this natural nutrient.

Breathing clean air is essential for optimal health. The quality of the air we breathe has a direct impact on our respiratory and cardiovascular systems, as well as our overall well-being. By taking steps to reduce our exposure to air pollution and support clean air initiatives, we can protect ourselves and our loved ones from the harmful effects of this pervasive problem.

Nurturing emotional well-being is essential for a healthy heart. Positive emotions, such as joy, gratitude, and contentment, have a protective effect on the cardiovascular system, while chronic stress, anxiety, and depression can increase the risk of heart disease and other health problems. By cultivating emotional well-being through mindfulness, exercise, healthy relationships, and other practices, we can nourish our hearts and promote overall health and happiness.

The pursuit of a spiritual connection is a deeply personal journey that can enhance our sense of meaning, purpose, and well-being. Whether it's through organized religion, nature, creative expression, or simply quiet contemplation, connecting with something larger than ourselves can provide a sense of peace, joy, and fulfillment.

Community plays a vital role in our well-being. Strong social connections provide a sense of belonging, support, and purpose. By building supportive relationships and engaging in shared experiences, we can foster a sense of community and enhance our overall health and happiness.

Sustainable living, a lifestyle choice that prioritizes the health of our planet, is not only an act of environmental stewardship but also a pathway to personal well-being. By making conscious choices that minimize our ecological footprint, we can create a healthier environment for ourselves and future generations.

In the journey toward optimal health, a naturopathic doctor can be an invaluable partner. NDs offer a holistic approach to health, addressing the root causes of disease and empowering patients to take an active role in their own healing. By partnering with an ND, you can tap into the wisdom of nature and unlock your body's innate capacity for health and vitality.

By embracing the principles of naturopathy and incorporating its practices into our lives, we can create a life that is not only healthy but also vibrant, joyful, and sustainable. We can rediscover our connection to nature, nurture our bodies and minds, and cultivate a deeper sense of meaning and purpose. Naturopathy offers a pathway to a life of well-being, a life that is in harmony with both ourselves and the natural world.

ᐳᐳᐳ

Citation And References

This book represents the culmination of extensive research and meticulous analysis, incorporating a diverse range of sources, including numerous books, scholarly studies, and personal experiences. Additionally, I have scoured various websites to gather relevant information and data essential for the compilation of this work. I have taken every precaution to ensure the accuracy of the information presented and have diligently cited all sources to acknowledge their contributions.

Despite these efforts, the possibility of inadvertent errors remains. I deeply value the insights of my readers and appreciate any feedback that can help identify and rectify such inaccuracies. I encourage you to bring any discrepancies to my attention.

Your feedback is not only welcome but crucial, as it will aid in correcting current editions and enhancing the content of future ones. I am committed to maintaining the highest standards of accuracy and reliability in my work and thank you for your support and understanding.

Additionally, I firmly uphold the principle of freedom of speech and expression as guaranteed under Article 19(1)(a) of the Constitution of India, and I respect the diverse viewpoints and expressions of all readers.

ppp

Other Books Of The Author

1. Empowering Minds: A Journey into Women's Self-Discovery and Power
2. The Dynamics of Motivation: Catalyzing Thought into Action
3. Meditation and Mental Well Being: The Path to Inner Peace and Clarity
4. The Psychology of Child Education: Nurturing Future Generations
5. Ethical Enlightenment: A Modern Guide to Living with Integrity
6. Voices of Empowerment: Stories of Women Rising Against Odds
7. Social Psychology in Everyday Life: Understanding Human Connections
8. The Essence of Motivational Speaking: Inspiring Change in Others
9. Balancing Acts: Women, Work, and the Will to Lead
10. Guiding with Grace: Raising Children with Compassion and Awareness
11. The Power of Positive Aging: Embracing Life After Fifty
12. Building Resilient Communities: Social Work in Action
13. The Ethical Educator: Principles for Teaching and Learning
14. From Insight to Impact: Social Psychology for a Better World
15. The Ethics of Empathy: A Guide to Ethical Living
16. The Science of Empowering the Self: Navigating Life's Challenges with Psychological Wisdom
17. The Mindful Conscious Leader: Meditation Techniques for Modern Management
18. Pioneering Spirit: Women's Pathways to Leadership and Empowerment
19. Feeling to Healing: The Role of Emotional Intelligence in Child Development
20. Transformative Talks and Words of Inspiration: Insights into Motivational Oratory

Bhajan

101. Pilgrimage of the Soul: Spiritual Journeys in India

ϷϷϷ

Contact

Dr. Minakshi Bansal
Social Activist
Ahmedabad, Gujarat, Bharat
minakshiindiag20@yahoo.com

ᏛᏛᏛ

|| LOKAHA SAMASTHAHA SUKHINO BHAVANTU ||